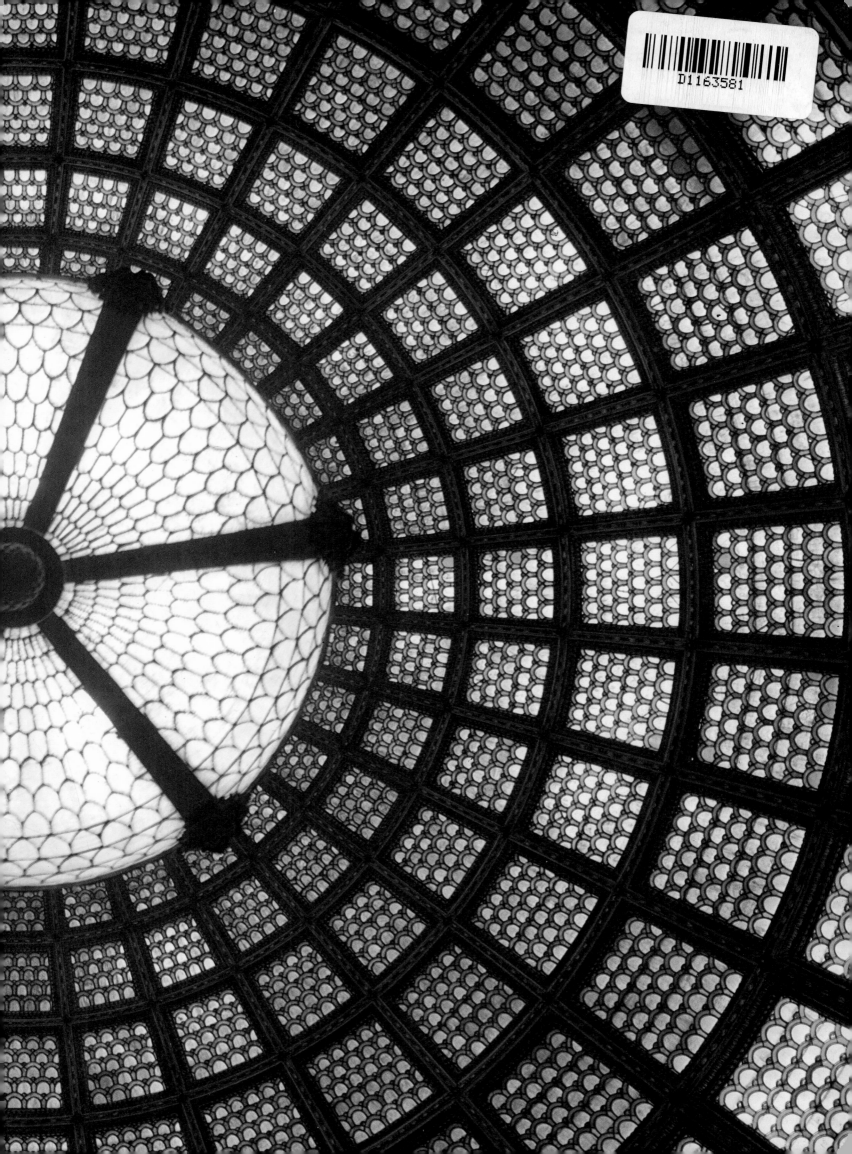

CHICAGO

Text by

Bill Harris

Designed and Produced by

Ted Smart & David Gibbon

MAYFLOWER BOOKS · NEW YORK CITY

DID someone say "second city"? Surely they can't mean Chicago!

Without Chicago, the city most Americans think of as "first" wouldn't have a skyline to brag about. It wouldn't have Dick Tracy to marvel at. Its citizens couldn't solve their problems by writing to "Dear Abby." Their Saturday nights wouldn't be as lively without John Belushi or Gilda Radner. They wouldn't have a Sears catalog to make their wishes come true. And where would they get their "New York cut" steaks?

Where, indeed! The only thing that makes Chicago "second" is its size. But it hasn't stopped growing since the days it was a stopping-off place on the way to China for adventurers on their way to find the Northwest Passage. And Chicago, remember, is still a youngster as the world's great cities go. It didn't officially become a city until 1837, the same year Victoria became England's Queen and certain cities on this side of the Atlantic were starting to talk about a thing called urban renewal.

But Chicago is far from an afterthought among American cities. It was an important spot to the Indians who, for generations, used it as a portage point to get their canoes across from the Illinois River to Lake Michigan. They called it "Chicagou" because of the huge number of wild onions that perfumed the air there.

A French Jesuit missionary, Peré Marquette, and a French Canadian explorer, Louis Jolliet, were the first white men to have found the spot. They arrived there in December, 1674, in the midst of a winter storm the likes of which makes today's Chicagoans proud of their flair for survival. Jolliet, displaying either a gift of prophecy or a flair for the obvious, wrote in his report to the Quebec Government that "It would only be necessary to make a canal by cutting through but half a league of prairie to pass from the foot of the lake of the Illinois to the River St. Louis which falls into the Mississippi. The bark, when there, would sail to the Gulf of Mexico."

Work on the canal didn't begin until 1836, when Chicago was already a booming town with so many immigrants there wasn't room enough for all of them to find a place to sleep. But they didn't seem to care, the town had its own brewery and eight taverns. And with work to be done on the canal, there was plenty to keep them busy during the day. It kept them busy for 12 years.

By the time the canal opened, Chicago had its first railroad, a 10-mile line called the Galena and Chicago Union. And a man named Cyrus Hall McCormick had already turned out 1,500 machines that took the hard work out of harvesting wheat. His factory gave work to hundreds and put Chicago on the map as a center for manufacturing. The new canal put the city ahead of New Orleans as the country's fastest-growing port. And the city fathers were predicting that 100,000 people would call Chicago home in 100 years. In spite of their enthusiasm

At the water's edge left, the Sun-Times building is a concrete reminder that Chicago is still probably the most competetive newspaper town in the world.

they underestimated the growth rate by more than three-and-a-half *million!* And in the 30-odd years since that century mark was passed, the population has doubled again.

Nothing is too fantastic to be believed in Chicago. Even today if a farmer's pretty young daughter wanders in off the prairie and meets up with a slick young fellow who twirls his moustache and says "I can get you into show business," she'd do well to listen. Long before Chicago had a canal and a bright future, an auction house had been converted into a theater they called the Rialto, and at least one of the saloons had a fine hall that was good enough for P. T. Barnum when he took his musical company there in 1840.

Dixieland jazz music would still be restricted to New Orleans cemeteries if it hadn't been taken up the river to be refined with a little Chicago style. In fact, every jazz style has found new ideas in Chicago and every jazz musician worthy of the name keeps the tradition alive there. The great Florenz Ziegfeld, a Chicago boy, got his first job in show business with Buffalo Bill, whose Wild West Show was playing the Academy of Music (of all places!) on Halsted Street. Bill himself had made his stage debut in Chicago in a play called "Scouts of the Prairie" written by the Chicagoan who had made Buffalo Bill famous in dime novels, Ned Buntline.

Chicago's audiences were enthusiastic, too. After Sarah Bernhardt stopped in Chicago on her first American tour, she said her time there was among "the most agreeable days since my arrival in America."

Vaudeville reached its flowering in Chicago years later when young men like Harry Herschfield took notes on the jokes they heard at places like Jacobs' Clark Street Theater and translated them to cartoons for the Chicago Daily News.

The media some say killed Vaudeville, radio and talking movies, was made possible by a young man named Lee De Forest who invented a thing he called a vacuum tube in a rooming house on Chicago's West Side.

Radio closed a lot of Vaudeville houses; movies gave them a reason to open again. What kept people home in the first place was programs like "Sam 'n' Henry," which was broadcast on WGN in 1925. The following year, they were lured over to WMAQ with the promise of nationwide exposure on a new radio network. *The Chicago Tribune,* owners of WGN, didn't like the loss much, especially since WMAQ belonged to the rival *Chicago Daily News.* The Trib sued, claiming it owned the name "Sam 'n' Henry." The court ruled the Tribune Company owned the name, but not the characters. So the characters, Freeman Gosden and Charles Correll, changed their names to "Amos 'n' Andy." At seven o'clock every evening for the next 20 years or more, the whole country turned its ear to Chicago to find out what was going on down at the Mystic Knights of the Sea Lodge Hall.

Radio kept people away from sporting events for a while, too. But thanks to the enthusiastic play-by-play announcing by men like Ronald Reagan, who was the voice of the Cubs around 1935, it eventually increased gate receipts at Wrigley Field.

When television came along with a threat to radio, Chicago, already a leading center of advertising, took to the new medium as naturally as it had to radio itself. Men like Dave Garroway, who had given radio an informal style that still infects disc jockeys all over the world, took Chicago's mood to TV and set the pattern that still exists on NBC's *Today* show, which he hosted during its first 10 years. At the same time, "Kukla, Fran and Ollie," broadcast every night from Chicago in television's early days, set the standard for hundreds of puppet shows on television right down through "Sesame Street".

And the beat goes on. Back in the late 1950's, a Chicago Chinese laundry was converted into a cabaret theater that was an important forum for topical comedians like Lenny Bruce. It was called Second City, and like so many Chicago institutions, it has become second to none in developing new talent. Mike Nichols and Elaine May were in one of its early graduating classes, so were David Steinberg, Robert Klein, Barbara Harris and Alan Arkin. If there's a thread of similarity among them, it's probably no coincidence. Call it Chicago style.

Its graduates today, John Belushi, Dan Ackroyd, Gilda Radner and others are the backbone of a new institution among America's young, television's "Saturday Night Live". It claims to originate from New York, but people who really understand know its origins are in Chicago.

Music and entertainment came to Chicago over an Indian trail in the heart of a man named Mark Beaubien who built the city's first hotel, which also happened to be the first building there that wasn't a log cabin. Old Mark was a fiddle player, and provided nightly music for his neighbors and guests to enjoy an evening of dancing. The evenings were great equalizers, with the town's leading professional men, often dancing with shopkeepers' daughters, doing some fancy sidesteps around the blanket-wrapped figures of hunters and trappers trying to get a little shut-eye on the floor in front of the fire.

In the mornings, Mrs Beaubien got the job of cleaning up. As if it wasn't enough work taking care of a family of 23 children and a hotel as well, the downstairs room every morning was a mud-splattered mess. If the music the night before had been lively enough, even the walls were covered with the stuff. It was a fact of life with every Chicago housewife in those days.

The site they had picked for their city had once been a swamp, and though they had drained it, they hadn't filled it in. Fort Dearborn was on high ground, and so was the South Side. They needed the fort to protect them from Indians, and the South Side was the site of a huge camp for wagon trains headed west. The tourists, then as now, were important for business, so the permanent residents were forced to live in the low spots where Mother Nature was doing her best to bring back the swamp.

They endured it, but never resigned themselves to it. All sorts of wild schemes were suggested to get rid of the muck, but the city stayed mired in it until the 1850's, when the wildest scheme of all was proposed. Why not, they said, just raise the center of the town by 10 or 12 feet? No matter that it was already a crowded city of 100,000 people. This was Chicago. They'll try anything in Chicago.

The first step was to tear down Fort Dearborn and spread the hill it had stood on along Randolph Street. It raised the level of the street some ten feet, and for the first time ladies could get to the Sherman House Hotel without getting their long skirts caked with mud.

More dirt was scraped away from the hills on the South Side and carted over to add stature to State Street and other thoroughfares that needed a boost. It was a lot of work, but well worth it. Everyone said so. Well, nearly everyone. One thing was wrong with the idea. When you raise the level of a street by ten feet, it's a problem getting into the front doors of the buildings that line it. And the problem was compounded by the fact that no one knew just how high any street would be raised. It all depended on how much dirt was available when the work was being done. Builders were forced to guess, and on many streets the level of the sidewalk varied two or three times in a single block. The inconvenience of the mud was replaced by the inconvenience of stairs to climb when you went out shopping or strolling. On top of that, it looked silly to have the city's important buildings peeking out at you from a hole in the ground. One of the great offenders was the Chicago Courthouse, but they solved the problem by adding an extra floor and a cupola to the top. When people built new houses on streets that were threatened with raising, they put a porch and a main entrance on the second floor. It became Chicago's first contribution to the architecture of America, and second floor porches were all the rage all over the country for a generation after.

But it wasn't always practical to add floors to existing buildings, or to tear them down and build new ones. There had to be a better answer.

The answer came to Chicago with a young man from New York named George Pullman.

Pullman had been an engineer on the construction of the Erie Canal. It had been a huge job connecting the Great Lakes with the Hudson River, and a lot of houses had to be moved to make way for it. When the canal was finished, Pullman was one of thousands who used it to go west to Chicago, and he arrived ready to go to work.

For his first trick, he decided to raise an entire block of four-story buildings at Lake and Wells Street, the busiest corner in town. He put 6,000 jacks under the row and hired 600 men to turn the screws. Every time a whistle blew, every screw was moved a half turn and timbers were tossed into the space under the buildings. The buildings were raised four feet in four days and all the while the cash registers kept ringing in the stores that were housed in them.

Flushed with success, he doubled the size of his crew and pushed the five-story Tremont Hotel six feet into the air without spilling a drop of soup in the hotel dining room.

While all that work was going on, Chicago's drugstore cowboys found a great new occupation for themselves. They took up positions next to the stairways that connected the multi-level sidewalks to catch sight of the ankles of the ladies hurrying up and down. In those days of long skirts, a trim ankle was a wonder to behold, and it was said that the women in Chicago had the trimmest ankles in the United States thanks to all that stair-climbing.

In spite of the fact that many of the streets and their buildings didn't match, and the architectural style of the city was a hodge-podge, Chicago in the '50s was as beautiful as it was exciting. Even the business district had trees along its streets, and most houses were set back from the streets behind wide lawns. There were flowers everywhere, both in town and on the prairie that stretched as far as the eye could see out from the edge of it. There were sunflowers taller than a man on horseback, asters as high as your head and flowers that competed with the rainbows that kept appearing out over the lake.

In the summer of 1871, rainbows were few and far between and the prairie flowers looked a little wilted by fall. Less than an inch of rain fell all summer long and forest fires were raging out of control up in Michigan and Wisconsin. By fall, people in Chicago were beginning to worry about their city. They had good reason to worry.

It started on the night of October 8. No one knows how, but it's convenient to blame a cow that allegedly kicked over a lantern and set the barn on fire. In fact, the barn on DeKoven Street may well have been where the fire began. Even if it wasn't, it was one of the first buildings to go.

During that first week of October, Chicago's tiny fire department had responded to more than 30 alarms, and on October 7 had spent 15 hours fighting a West Side blaze that destroyed some $750,000 worth of property. At 9:15 on the night of the 8th, the watchman in the tower at City Hall saw flames just to the north and sounded the alarm. The firemen had no sooner harnessed their horses when an alarm came in placing the fire in an entirely different spot. But the watchman didn't change his opinion, nor did he change his instructions that sent the wrong company to respond. By the time they raced more than a mile to get there, DeKoven Street was completely engulfed in flames and the fire was spreading. In less than two hours, it became two fires when it jumped the river and started to spread over the South Side. By then, people from every part of town were heading west as fast as their legs or their frightened horses could carry them. The gas works had already blown up and the only light to show them the way was the red glow in the sky that must have seemed like the end of the world itself.

The problem was compounded when a bus company stable at the edge of the business district caught fire, and firemen were forced to fight three separate fires at the same time. Some companies gave up on the West Side and went south where the fire was spreading fast along both sides of the business district.

Meanwhile, fire departments in Milwaukee and Saint Louis, Cincinnati and even New York loaded apparatus onto railroad cars bound for Chicago, where elegant new hotels, retail stores, office buildings, factories and homes were being destroyed in the fire, which was so intense that even the smoke from it was consumed in the flames.

Twenty-five hours after it started, a light rain stopped the spread of the flames and another day later, people began to drift back to count their losses. Just about everything was destroyed in an area of more than 2,000 acres, some four square miles, compared with 500 acres of destruction in the Great Fire of London. More than 18,000 buildings were gone, including the homes of more than 100,000 persons. At least 300 died in the fire, but, significantly, no one dreamed of writing a death notice for Chicago herself.

Even before the coal that had been stored in basements stopped burning, one Chicagoan built a wooden shack on Washington Street. He hoisted a sign over the door that identified it as a real estate office and added another next to it that said: "All gone, except wife, children and energy".

The Chicago Tribune, which hit what was left of the streets by October 12, began its lead editorial: "All is not lost!" The piece ended with the inspiring challenge: "Let the watchword henceforth be, Chicago shall rise again".

All over town people reacted the same way. As one of them explained, they believed that "Chicago will have more men, more money, more business within five years than she would have had without the fire". It was a chance to start fresh and to avoid mistakes all of them had made before. Best of all, it was an opportunity to get their stores, houses and streets all on the same level.

They started rebuilding with a passion that can only be called fanatical. And the enthusiasm hasn't stopped yet. Chicago became the birthplace of modern architecture, and though all the world has copied her buildings, the original is still the undisputed best.

One of the most enterprising of the architects who went to work after the fire was John M. Van Osdel who advertised that he was prepared to design "plain wholesale stores and warehouses . . . plain dwellings and public buildings, court or school houses". He would also do work in Gothic, Norman or Romanesque style, but was forced to charge more for that. His one surviving building in the city is one that also survived the fire thanks to its location, the Holy Family Church on West Roosevelt.

Just before the fire, Van Osdel had supervized the renovation of the Palmer House Hotel, and when the fire broke out, he buried his plans and records under the hotel cellar. Days later, he dug them up, perfectly preserved in the glazed clay.

It gave him faith in an idea for fireproofing that's still used. On his first big commission, for the Kendall Building, he specified hollow tile floor arches, proposed by New York builder George H. Johnson, and terra cotta walls. It had never been done before. But then, the world hadn't been quite as ready for a fireproof building before.

Other business people went back to work with gusto, too. Marshall Field reopened his store within days in an old horse barn. The fancy houses along Michigan Avenue below the burned-out area were converted into stores by their owners whose regular establishments had vanished. And to keep their community standing intact, men like

George Pullman and W. W. Kimball built palatial mansions along Prairie Avenue. It was there the new Chicago society was formed around exclusive clubs like the Calumet, the Union and the Illinois. It wasn't enough to be able to afford the $100 initiation fee and $80 annual dues. You had to *be* somebody. And to be somebody of importance in 19th century Chicago was to be somebody with a future. It was clearly a place on the move.

To show the direction they were moving, the owner of the International Harvester Company brought H.H. Richardson, the best architect of the day, from Boston to build him a house that would be a symbol of his position. The building, which is now the headquarters of the Chicago School of Architecture Foundation, is sturdy, solid, serene and impressive. Just what the doctor ordered. Marshall Field was so impressed by Richardson's Romanesque flair, he hired him to build a store and warehouse that would impress the world. It impressed Chicago anyway. Though Richardson died before he added any more structures to the new Chicago skyline, imitations of his work appeared everywhere and for more than 10 years nothing much was built of any importance that didn't have at least some touches of Richardson's ideas.

But, of course, Chicago's architects had ideas of their own. Among them was the idea that with steel frames buildings could go on forever. The sky's the limit, they said. And they began to build skyscrapers.

It was easy to understand the concept of building with steel beams, especially in Chicago where nearby steel mills were turning out beams for bridges. And their influential owners smelled a terrific new market for their product. But there were others, who hadn't forgotten all that mud, who said that while it may be a good idea, it was a terrible one for a city built on a swamp.

Architect William Jenney was first to take the leap forward by building a structure for the Home Insurance Company around an iron cage. People were impressed when it didn't fall down. Other builders were impressed by how fast it went up. The idea was clearly here to stay. But buildings still had to be built on pilings in a marshy place like Chicago. Another innovation was needed if buildings were really going to scrape the sky.

John Root, of the firm of Burnham and Root, had an idea that would make it all possible. In his design for the Montauk Block, built in 1882 at Dearborn and Monroe Streets, he built a huge concrete raft, reinforced with railroad ties to distribute the weight of the building over a large area rather than on narrow pilings. Some of his so-called friends suggested the raft would be good to move the building out into the lake if fire should break out again. But thanks to Root's innovation, the Montauk, though only ten stories high, was the first skyscraper worthy of the name. And it started a trend that eventually made Chicago the site of the tallest building in the world.

The Montauk was torn down in 1902, apparently without a tear from anyone. Some years after it had been built, a friend told Root he didn't care for the building; to which the architect replied, "who in hell does?"

A Burnham and Root building everyone cares very much for is still standing on South LaSalle Street. It's known as The Rookery because it replaced a temporary city hall and water tower that had become the most popular spot in town for Chicago's pigeon flock. It was typical of Root to keep the name for the new building, which is a monument to a man who was obviously cheerful and good-humored.

It's easily the happiest place in town, with a courtyard that gives just about every tenant natural light and a view of some of the airiest cast iron work anywhere. It's covered with a cast iron and glass dome that was a marvel of its day and is still a joy to behold nearly a century later. There have been some improvements made in the Rookery, including Frank Lloyd Wright's decoration of the courtyard. But the building works as well for the 20th century as it did for the 19th. Just walking through the front door perks up your spirits. No wonder it's been fully rented since that front door was first opened in 1886.

All that building lured all the best builders to Chicago, and probably the very best was a young Bostonian named Louis Sullivan. More than anything else, Sullivan passionately believed that the idea of democracy depended more on the quality of a country's buildings than on its statesmen. And he preached his gospel with buildings that were designed for people to use and enjoy. "A building is an act," he said, and he showed what he meant in structures like the old Stock Exchange Building at 30 North LaSalle Street and the Carson, Pirie, Scott department store.

His strong beliefs were passed on to a young man he had hired as a design assistant, Frank Lloyd Wright. His ideas also inspired Mies van der Rohe. And through them, Le Corbusier, Walter Gropius and others took the message from Chicago to the rest of the world. By the beginning of the 20th century, modern architecture was a fact of life everywhere, and it all began on the shores of Lake Michigan.

Before Louis Sullivan, most American architects were European-trained, and their work generally European-inspired. With the establishment of the Chicago School of architecture, the shoe was on the other foot. When Sullivan designed a tower, he said "every inch of it should be tall. The force and power of altitude should be in it". When he designed a horizontal structure, he gave it the spirit of the prairie, an inspiration that Frank Lloyd Wright turned into a very fine art in a host of Chicago houses. In every case, the human factor was the function their forms followed. It was to be Chicago's gift to the world, and even though lesser people in other places have sometimes misinterpreted the message, anyone can find it alive and well on the streets of Chicago.

But old ideas die hard, and when Chicago decided to show herself off to the world with the Columbian Exposition in 1893, the local architects naturally wanted the fair's buildings to reflect their new ideas. A more socially prominent group of designers from New York overruled them in favor of a classical theme. Sullivan predicted it would set American architecture back fifty years. But there had been argument enough already. When the idea of a fair was first proposed, politicians in New York and Washington worked hard to make their cities the site. In fact, it was during the debate that Charles Dana wrote in the New York *Sun* that no one should listen to "the nonsensical claims of the windy city." And that was the first time anyone had ever called Chicago "windy." Chicago won the battle, of course, and even if its architects felt they had lost the war, it promised to be a grand spectacle. The plans were so grand, in fact, the opening had to be put off for a year to get the buildings built. Which is why the 400th anniversary of the discovery of America was celebrated in the four hundred and first year.

It was well worth the wait. The "White City" of classical buildings covered more than 600 acres of what had been a marsh on the shore of the lake. The dome on the administration building was higher, and everyone agreed much grander, than the Capitol in Washington. The fountain in front of it spewed out enough water every day to put out the Chicago fire. The fine arts building, since rebuilt in stone to become the Museum of Science and Industry, was touted as the greatest structure built by man since the Parthenon. The manufacturing building was the biggest in the world at the time, and it was said the great pyramid could be put on display inside it with plenty of room left over for the mobs of visitors lured to Chicago for the show.

At night, the whole thing was lit by the greatest collection of electric lights that had ever been brought together in one place. The spectacle was described in a book written soon after the fair as a "wealth of coloring".

"The climax of all the brilliant display," it said, "is the electric fountains at the head of the lagoon in front of the administration building. Here are light effects of surpassing loveliness in rich varying hues; sprays, jets and columns of water appearing as though ablaze in the glow of these powerfu! electric currents. . . . Nearby gondolas and electric launches speed swiftly to and fro across the lagoon, breaking its resplendent surface into a thousand glittering fragments, while from the plaza strains of music are wafted into the still night air".

Some of the music was provided by John Philip Sousa and his band, but far and away the most popular music at the fair wafted through the flaps of a tent that housed an attraction everyone in the country was talking about; a girl called Little Egypt. They said that when she danced, you could see every muscle in her body at the same time. And the electric thrill that she created was a lot more fun than a bunch of electric lights or even the giant dynamo in the Electricity Hall.

The fair was an uplifting cultural experience, too. Bach's clavichord was there for all to see; so was the contract Columbus had negotiated with Ferdinand and Isabella. But the biggest uplift of all came from an invention of a Pittsburgh bridge-builder named George Ferris. It was two 320-foot wheels set 30 feet apart with carriages between them big enough to hold 40 people each. During the single summer of the big show, 1,750,000 people stood in line to take the 20-minute ride.

If they had time left over, they could see Gentleman Jim Corbett demonstrate how he knocked out the great John L. Sullivan in the fight ring. Or they could marvel at the strength of the Great Sandow, the strongest man in the world. If they wanted to get that strong themselves, Bernarr Macfadden had an exercise machine to show them how.

In downtown Chicago, Lillian Russell, a home-town girl, was playing at the Columbia Theater, and her constant companion, Diamond Jim Brady, became another attraction for people who didn't mind telling you they had mortgaged their farms for a chance to see this once-in-a-life time show.

In a flush of enthusiasm before the fair opened, the new Mayor of Chicago, Carter Harrison, told the world that he had bought 200 barrels of whiskey to entertain his constituents and friends during the festivities. "It's good Chicago whiskey," he said, "the kind that can kill at the distance of a mile". He let it be known that his latchstring was always out, and everybody was welcome to stop by for a sip or two.

On one of the last days of the fair, Mayor's Day in fact, a man with a gun came to the door, and that was the end of Mayor Harrison. But down at the club-house everyone had to admit his last days were great days. The world knew now what Chicago was capable of doing. Theodore Dreiser was as impressed as anyone. "Out of nothing in this dingy city," he wrote, "which but a few years before had been a wilderness of wet grass and mud flats had now been reared this vast and harmonious collection of perfectly constructed buildings containing in their delightful interiors the artistic, mechanical and scientific achievements."

All Chicago was bursting with pride. And with good reason.

With a population over the million-and-a-half mark, the city was already the second biggest in the country. It was served by ten railroads, boasted the fastest streetcars in the country, had an elevated railroad right in the heart of the business district and factories everywhere. Naturally, that meant Chicago was a bustling place. Smoky, too. It was quite possibly a place only a native could love. Rudyard Kipling thought so, anyway. He said, "having seen it, I urgently desire never to see it again. It is inhabited by savages. I spent ten hours in that huge wilderness wandering through scores of miles of those terrible streets, and jostling some few hundred thousand of these terrible people who talk money through their noses.

"I listened to people who said that the mere fact of spiking down strips of iron to wood and getting a steam and iron thing to run along them was progress."

Kipling, remember, had been to Calcutta and wrote nice things about it. So much for taste! On the same visit, he toured the stockyards where he was impressed by a woman butcher:

"She stood in a patch of sunlight, the red blood under her shoes, the vivid carcasses stacked around her, a bullock bleeding its life away not six feet from her and the death factory roaring all around her. She looked curiously with hard, bold eyes and was not ashamed."

He left town right after that and was never seen in Chicago again.

But other writers saw a different Chicago. "Just to be part of it makes me crazy with life," wrote Dreiser. And Chicago has probably produced more good writers than any other American city. The list runs from Carl Sandburg and Eugene Field to Ernest Hemingway and James T. Farrell. Edgar Rice Burroughs created "Tarzan" in Oak Park. And, coincidentally, the character was made famous in the movies by a Chicago athlete named Johnny Weissmuller. Edgar Lee Masters was practicing law in Chicago when his "Spoon River Anthology" was first published.

Then why does everybody think of Chicago as a city full of gangsters? Why do first time visitors look for Claire Trevor and George Raft when they stroll down Michigan Avenue?

It seems to have begun when the 20th century began. Around that time, a London newspaper reported that "other places hide their blackness out of sight, Chicago treasures it in the heart of the business district and gives it a veneer."

The business district they were writing about was the First Ward, a section of town they called "the Levee". You could get anything at all on the Levee, including a bump on your head and an empty wallet. They say there were more than 200 brothels in the neighbourhood, and the place got its name from the incredible number of Southern gamblers who set up shop there. The "in" spot was a saloon run by Ike Bloom, who made more money from his girls than from his drinks, and made it a point to get his name into the papers as often as possible to make sure his joint stayed the "in" spot.

Other brothels were very posh and lured new business with elaborate brochures distributed in the better parts of town. It was during a visit to one of them by Prince Henry of Prussia that one of the girls, in her enthusiasm, kicked off her slipper which knocked over a glass of champagne. When the Prince saw the champagne-filled slipper, he said, "the poor dear shouldn't get her feet wet," and proceeded to drink a toast with it.

Every man in the room followed his example, and at that moment Chicago gave the world yet another quaint custom.

The same bordello was also the center of one of the great scandals of Chicago history. But how it happened, or whether it happened at all, is still a mystery, as well as a testament to the way rumors work. Naturally, if it was the sort of place royalty patronized, it wasn't much loved by the other madames in the Levee. According to the story, a prominent member of a Chicago family died in one of them and its alert owner had her minions carry the corpse to her competitor's establishment with orders to stuff the body into the furnace. Then she picked up the phone and called the police. But in the meantime, her potential victim had been warned and had a pair of her strongarm men load

the body into a taxi and accompany it home. Over the years, the identity of the dead man kept changing and the tale embellished. Hardly any of the leading families of the city escaped having it told about them. And every time the story was told, most people believed it because the Levee was a very popular place for young men from every segment of society.

The neighborhood was represented at City Hall by a pair of aldermen named Hinky Dink Kenna and Bathhouse John Coughlin. Together they kept the climate cool, so to speak, for a price. Their partnership lasted nearly fifty years, during which time they built a fortune. It was said that Bathhouse was the best-dressed man in America. It was said best by The Bath himself when someone compared him to the Prince of Wales. "When it comes to mapping out style for well-dressed Americans," he shot back, "the Prince is simply a faded two-spot in the deck of fashion."

Hinky Dink was no slouch, either. But as a believer in thrift, he saved for the future. He did take a trip to Europe once, and when he got back, the best comment he could make about Rome was that "most everybody there has been dead 2,000 years".

Hink had a lot of Italian constituents in the First Ward, and he knew they were very much alive. Big Jim Colosimo was a restaurant owner who had lured the likes of Enrico Caruso to the Levee to sample his spaghetti. On the side, he sold "protection" to the bordello owners, which was much more profitable than spaghetti. Though Hinky Dink Kenna preferred to rub elbows with the Irish in the Ward, he was nothing if not a practical man, and he made a deal with Big Jim. Now he had the best of both worlds. With his cadre of drunks and bums who turned out on election day and Colosimo's enforcers who could keep the Ward in line, he had both power and respectability. What more could a politician want?

In lesser men, more power would be the answer. But both Hink and The Bath had decided as young men that the best way to stay out of jail was to stay small. "We leave Washington graft to the Congressmen," one of them said. "There's less risk in the small stuff and in the long run, it pays a damn sight more."

Their proudest moment was the annual First Ward Ball, a fund-raising effort for the local Democratic organization. It was Bathhouse John's idea in the first place, and he put himself into it with single-minded enthusiasm. He even wrote the music for the bands to play, including such immortal hits as "Why Did They Build The Lake So Near The Shore?" and "They're Tearing Up Clark Street Again".

All the business people in the Ward, from saloon keepers to bordello owners, had the arm put on them to buy blocks of tickets. Brewers and distillers were expected to make donations to the bar as well. And waiters paid Bathhouse John for the privilege of working the frolic.

The most spectacular ball of them all was the one they staged in 1908. Bathhouse John showed up dressed in a tuxedo with purple lapels and a bright red sash. The hatcheck girl, who had tipped *him,* got to hang up his yellow overcoat and red scarf and took special care not to lose his pink kid gloves. The working girls from the Levee didn't show up until after their work was over, of course. But it was worth the wait because they came in costume. The most popular effect was an Egyptian look, obviously a holdover from the Centenniel Exposition. But whatever the costume, short skirts were the common denominator. The *Tribune* said that was because ". . . it was bad form to wear anything that might collect germs from the floor."

There were plenty of fights, lots of song-singing and some 15,000 uninvited guests tried to get in on the fun by breaking down the doors. But The Bath had anticipated that, and in addition to a special police detail, he hired 200 bouncers to help keep order. It was so crowded with paying guests, one newspaperman said, ". . . even those already drunk were forced to stand erect".

Hinky Dink's assessment of the party was, "It's a lollapalooza! . . . Chicago ain't no sissy town".

By the end of 1908, Chicagoans were a little weary of the shenanigans in the First Ward, but the man who decided to do something about it was an Englishman who had gone to Chicago for the Columbian Exposition and decided to stay a while. William T. Stead wrote a little book he called "If Christ Came to Chicago! A Plea For The Union of All Who Love in the Service of All Who Suffer." The first printing sold out in the first week, and Stead was on his way toward reforming Chicago. He attacked everything Chicagoans held sacred, from wide-open vice to aldermen who considered it their natural right to earn at least $25,000 a year on the side by selling votes. His book quoted chapter and verse on the city's vice operations, and that, of course, was the key to its success. People were buying it to get all the juicy details.

But many got the message, and it seemed the days of the likes of Blubber Bob Gray, Dago Frank Lewis and Snapper Johnny Malloy were clearly numbered.

Not long after the 1908 First Ward Ball, another Englishman, an evangelist named Gypsy Smith, led some 5,000 followers through the streets of the Levee behind a band playing "Where He Leads Me, I Will Follow." It was easy to hear the music because word had gone out in the district to keep things quiet while "the reverend" was passing through. Once he had passed, though, it was business as usual again. But business would never be the same again.

The city's newspapers, which had been severely chided in Stead's book, began reporting what was really going on. Chicago's newspapers are among the best in the world, and this was their finest hour. Their stories couldn't be ignored, and resulted in citizens' organizations that brought pressure on City Hall. In a move that surprised everyone in the Levee, the Mayor closed down the most famous brothel. Within a year, he had shut down the whole neighborhood in actions that killed his political career. But the Levee went with him and Chicago went to work to change its image.

The city had more than enough resources to do the job. Back East, a man named Tom Edison had just invented pictures that moved, and plenty of Chicagoans had ideas that could make them more fun when they did. In the early part of the 20th century, more movies were made in Chicago than anywhere, and it was on the prairies outside of town that somebody first headed off somebody else at the pass in cowboy pictures.

Newspapermen like Carl Sandburg, Ben Hecht and Ring Lardner turned to more serious ideas, and the rest of the country sat up and took notice. Down in Baltimore, H. L. Mencken said, "Find a writer who is indubitably an American in every pulsebeat, snort and adenoid, an American who has something new and peculiarly American to say and who says it in an unmistakable American way and nine times out of ten you will find that he has some sort of connection with the gargantuan and inordinate abattoir by Lake Michigan . . . that he was bred there, or got his start there, or passed through there in the days when he was young and tender. In Chicago, a spirit broods upon the face of the waters."

They called it Chicago's Golden Age. And in every quarter of the arts from jazz music to poetry, Chicago was clearly the place to be.

It was also the time Chicago picked up its tradition of being America's number one convention city. In 1912, the Republicans met there to nominate William Howard Taft as their presidential candidate. Former President Teddy Roosevelt showed up to try getting the nomination for himself, and the fight was one of the great spectacles in the history of American politics. Roosevelt lost, but before he left Chicago he formed a new party and ran anyway. The oratory, the drama, the lure of a good fight all combined to keep Chicago in the spotlight, and it's been the first choice of imaginative convention planners ever since.

During the risorgimento, many of the people who had made the Levee lively either retired or went into other less flamboyant businesses. But some of them, of course, were too old to learn new trades.

Among them was Big Jim Colosimo. Jim just went underground. That made him a target for potential rivals, so he went to New York and hired a bodyguard, a young fellow named Johnny Torrio. Torrio was as smart as he was tough, and it was only a matter of time before he was bigger than his boss. In a stroke of marketing genius, Torrio reasoned that the automobile would take business away from the central city, and talked Big Jim into giving him the suburban territory. By 1912, places like Calumet City, Hammond and Cicero were Torrio country, with a string of roadhouses where a steel worker on his way home could get just about anything at all.

It kept Torrio so busy, he forgot one day that he was Big Jim's bodyguard. And that was the end of Big Jim.

Torrio took over, of course, and now he needed a bodyguard and a good right hand. He found both in the person of another New Yorker who called himself Al Brown. Early in his career, a Chicago newspaper identified him as Alfred Caponi. But it wasn't long before they got it right, it was Alphonse Capone.

They didn't come any tougher. Any kid who had grown up on the streets of New York's lower East Side with a name like Alphonse had to be tough.

When he arrived in Chicago, he bought an old fishbowl, a couple of chairs, a piano and other assorted junk and opened a second-hand furniture store on South Wabash Avenue. There is no record whether he ever sold any of the stuff. Some years later, when the Federal Government charged him with income tax evasion, they based their claim on an income of $1,050,000 between 1924 and 1929. They were just guessing, of course. And the guess was clearly conservative. At one point during the trial, the judge was offered a million-and-a-half in cash to let Al go free.

Part of his success came from the Federal Government itself. In 1920, the same year Capone went to Chicago, the drinking and selling of alcoholic beverages in America became illegal. What an opportunity!

Torrio began buying breweries and raised the price of his product to $50 a barrel. Before long, he had a monopoly on the brewery business, and the price went up. But, of course, getting the monopoly was a bloody business. Their chief competition came from a North State Street florist named Dion O'Banion, the most powerful man in Chicago. O'Banion controlled the wealthiest and most fashionable parts of the city; politicians, speakeasies, gambling dens, the works.

Torrio, Capone and O'Banion together had become too big for anybody, on either side of the law, to touch. But even Chicago wasn't big enough for all that power and ambition.

One day, while O'Banion was cutting chrysanthemums for a funeral bouquet, a big blue car pulled up in front of his shop. Three men got out and went inside. One of them shook the florist's hand, and before he could say "good morning", six shots rang out. Five were quick and straight to O'Banion's chest. Then the handshaker released his grip and fired the sixth, a grace shot, into O'Banion's head.

The funeral that followed was one of the biggest Chicago had ever seen. A special casket was shipped from New York for the occasion. Lined with solid silver and bronze, it had a plate glass cover. The inscription on the base said "suffer the little children to come unto me". There were 26 truckloads of flowers, including a basket of roses signed, "from Al".

Capone and Torrio showed up at the graveside along with Bugs Moran and Hymie Weiss and others who suspected they were the killers and were looking for revenge. As soon as the funeral was over, Torrio vanished from sight with O'Banion's men hot on his trail. They followed him all the way to Cuba, then back to Chicago, where they shot him on the front porch of his home. Now it was up to Al Capone.

The war for control lasted four years. During that time a lot of people died and a lot of other people blamed Al Capone. As he himself put it, "I've been accused of every death except the casualty list of the World War".

His arch enemies by now were the six Genna brothers, who had a Government permit to operate a plant for industrial alcohol. Much of the product they distilled was drinkable. It was smalltime stuff, though. To increase production, they sent word back to their native Sicily that they would provide apartments and an income of $15 a day for families that agreed to keep stills in the apartments. More than 100 families took them up on the offer and the Gennas opened a warehouse on State Street to keep the public supplied. It was the biggest store on the street at the time, and the Gennas got very rich indeed.

In the space of a few short weeks, three of the brothers were gunned down and word went out that the other three were marked for death, too. To avoid it, they went home to Sicily, and now all Capone had to worry about was Bugs Moran and the remnants of the O'Banion gang.

The war started when eight carloads of men drove up to Capone's headquarters at the Hawthorne Hotel in Cicero and fired a thousand bullets into the lobby. Not a single bullet hit anyone. One of the survivors told police, "It wasn't no gang fight. A stick-up, that's all. They wanted my roll."

The war ended in a truce after a black Packard pulled up in front of a Clark Street Garage on February 14, 1929. Five men, three dressed in police uniforms, went inside. One of the seven men there is reputed to have said, "Wassa matter? You ain't to be paid until the end of the month."

He didn't have time to say much more. A machine gun at knee height and another at chest height cut all seven down. Then the three "policemen" walked the other two at gunpoint to the waiting Packard and drove away. When the real police arrived, one of the victims, not quite dead yet, was asked who had done this thing. "No one done it," he said. "No one shot me."

Of course, the whole world thought Al Capone had ordered the massacre, as it was called, and it brought him international fame as well as control of Chicago. And what made this killing more dramatic than the others? An innocent bystander, a visitor to the garage, was caught in the crossfire. And with that, people began to demand that something be done.

Within a few years, something was done. Capone was sentenced to 11 years in prison and required to pay $70,000 in fines and costs. The charge was income tax-evasion. It was a "blow below the belt," he said. "I have never heard of anyone getting more than five years for income tax trouble, but they are prejudiced against me. I never had a chance."

Before he died in prison, he was heard to say, "If I'd known what I was stepping into in Chicago, I never would have left the Five Points outfit (in New York)."

If Valentine's Day, 1929 is of any importance to Chicago's history, what happened there on the same day eight years before is just as important. On February 14, 1921, readers of *The Chicago Tribune* were informed that one of their close friends, Walt Wallet of Gasoline Alley had found a baby boy on his doorstep. He named him Skeezix, and every Sunday for three generations, people all over America watched Skeezix grow up, and Walt get older. The boy in the comic strip eventually became a father himself, even a grandfather. And although the actual location of their neighborhood was never officially identified as Chicago, the people who inspired it were ordinary citizens of Chicago, and there wasn't a gangster among them.

Dick Tracy comes from Chicago, too. And Buck Rogers first saw the future there. The Toonerville Trolley rattled and rolled off a Chicago drawing board. And it was in a Chicago office that Winnie Winkle did her thing as the "breadwinner". The list of comic strip characters born in Chicago is almost endless, running from Smitty to Little Orphan Annie, and including Moon Mullins and Steve Canyon. And the list isn't restricted to comic strips. Both Ann Landers and "Dear Abby" are Chicagoans, for instance. The first major newspaper syndicate was founded in Chicago in 1865, when Anson Kellogg sold articles as well as advertising to almost 1,500 newspapers all over the country. It was big business then, and it still is. And Chicago is right at the heart of it.

The heart of Chicago is the rectangle formed by Wabash, Wells, Lake and Van Buren Streets they call The Loop. It got its name from a band of elevated railroad tracks that branched out from there to other parts of the city. It's the place to be if you don't want to miss the beauty and bustle of Chicago.

From the center of it, you can see the Federal Center, possibly Mies Van Der Rohe's best work. Turn your heard, and there is the Marquette Building, one of the first in the world with a steel skeleton. Over a bit, the tallest bank building in the world, the First National, with one of the liveliest plazas in town. Down the street is the Monadnock, once the biggest office building anywhere, and still a solid monument to the builders of the 1890's. And further down, the joyful Rookery. Off in the distance, but not too far, is the world's tallest building, the Sears Tower. You can feel all the excitement without taking a single step!

Walk a little south and experience the Auditorium Building, Louis Sullivan's combination hotel, office building and theater. If it reminds you a little of Radio City Music Hall in New York, it's probably no coincidence. But this one's the original.

Over on South Michigan Avenue, you get an idea of what Louis Sullivan meant when he said a skyscraper should be "every inch tall". His Gage Building is all that, and much more. And across the street, a structure that's every inch a beauty, the Art Institute of Chicago.

Across the Michigan Avenue Bridge, the street is known as "The Magnificent Mile". The reason is that no word but "magnificent" does it justice. Anyone who has any feeling at all about the beauty of cities simply has to rate it among the best urban landscapes in the world.

It begins magnificently with the Wrigley Building on one side and the Tribune Tower on the other. The facade of the Trib Tower is laced with hunks of stone from famous structures all over the world, but the building doesn't need it at all. The competition for the design of it, won by Raymond Hood, set the style for buildings all over America in the 1930's, including such work as Rockefeller Center in New York.

The street itself is separated from the art galleries and stores that line it by wide strips of grass and trees, just as the whole city was in the beginning. Saks Fifth Avenue is there, so are Gucci and Tiffany. And not far up, standing like a jewel in a crown, the Water Tower, which, along with the pumping station across from it, was the only thing left standing after the great fire.

It gives its name to one of the most unusual buildings in Chicago, Water Tower Place. Inside, the lower floors are a great urban shopping mall with Marshall Fields and Lord & Taylor as the centerpiece and other stores including F. A. O. Schwartz and Rizzoli International Bookstore, plus restaurants, two movie theaters and a legitimate theater. You get from one level to another in glass-enclosed elevators that rise up through an atrium with as much greenery as the Amazon jungle. If shopping wears you out, the upper floors of the building house the Ritz-Carlton, a great hotel, even by Chicago standards, which have been remarkably high since the city was a stop for wagon trains headed west.

Big John is right across the street, the 100-story John Hancock Center, a combination office building and apartment house. Its huge steel crossmembers are a constant reminder that this is indeed a windy city. Behind it, the Playboy Building is a reminder that this is a city in tune with the times. Even Americans who disapprove have to admit that the magazine and the empire connected with it that's housed in this building has done more to influence American attitudes in the 20th century than almost any other institution.

The searchlight on top of it, the Lindbergh Light, named not for his flight to Paris, but for his hundreds of trips from St. Louis to Chicago as a mail pilot, was once a beacon for airplanes and for ships on the lake. When the Hancock Center was built, the light kept tenants awake all night, and so today the beacon never shines south.

The Magnificent Mile ends, but the Gold Coast begins, at the Drake Hotel. It's one of the most perfect residential neighborhoods in the city with well-scaled buildings that offer views of the lake and its beaches. It's peaceful and elegant, but exciting, too.

But almost anyone under 30 will tell you that the real excitement in Chicago is in Old Town, not far from Lincoln Park. It's a lively collection of shops and jazz joints, fast food shops and craft stores surely aimed at the young, not the old. It's a trendy place that changes almost every week as trends come and go. But one thing's sure, if it's new, it's in Old Town, and that by itself is worth a trip.

You see plenty of young people on the South Side of Chicago, too. It's where you'll find the University of Chicago, the place where the atomic bomb was first developed, but more justly famous as one of the world's great universities.

The campus is as beautiful as any that class themselves in the "ivy league", and its graduates have distinguished themselves as a league by themselves. And at the edge of the campus is a house that has become one of the few to have been named a national landmark by dint of its beauty alone, Frank Lloyd Wright's Robie House. Among other innovations we take for granted in houses today, this 1909 gem was the first house in the world built on a concrete slab. It was the first to have an attached garage, first to have indirect lighting, and that was the first to be controlled by dimmer switches.

There are four other Wright houses in the same neighborhood, but Oak Park and River Forest are where his Prairie Houses were developed, and between them, they have 31 to show off, including his own house and studio on Chicago Avenue.

Oak Park and River Forest, like Glenview and Lincolnwood, are small towns outside the city limits. But going from one to the other, you can hardly tell the difference, because all Chicago is a collection of neighborhoods, each different from the one next to it, each with a personality all its own.

Up on the Northwest Side, there are more Gypsies than in any other American city. There are more Lithuanians on the South Side than anywhere else in the country. And, as was proudly pointed out when Pope John Paul II visited Chicago, there are more Poles here than in any city in the world except Warsaw.

The Chinese along Clark Street, the Sicilians and Ukranians on Chicago Avenue, the Swedes in Andersonville all live in the same neighborhoods their parents found warm and welcoming when they arrived in Chicago looking for a new lease on life. Taking a tour of Chicago's neighborhoods is like taking a trip around the world.

Then who in the world had the nerve to call it "second city"? The perpetrator is a writer named A. J. Liebling, who coined the phrase in a series of articles in *The New Yorker* Magazine. As soon as the first of them appeared, he said he started getting mail accusing him of trying to start a "be nasty to Chicago" club. He later wrote that the loudest protests of all ". . . came from the suburbs; the people who wouldn't live in the city if you gave them the place." That

was in the early 1950s, when all America seemed to be turning its back on its cities in favor of a little place in the country.

Happily, the trend has been reversed by now, and cities have become fashionable again. Interestingly, Chicago has never been anything but fashionable, and it's been known for more than a generation as "the city that works." It's big, and it has all the big problems other cities do. But it has a small town quality to it, too, and that's one of the things that makes it work.

It's a solid, hard-working place, probably more American than any other place in America. It stretches out 25 miles to the north and south and 15 miles west from the lake. Up and down the lake shore, it's as exciting and cosmopolitan as any city in the world. But just a few blocks from the shore, it suddenly becomes a quiet, small town with a human scale most cities envy. Senator Paul Douglas summed it up when he said "Chicago is a town with a Queen Anne front and a Mary Anne back."

At night, the streets downtown are safer than in most other American cities, and possibly more exciting than any other. And, yes, the natives are friendly. They're proud, too. And why not? There's plenty to be proud of in Chicago . . . it has the world's biggest airport, its tallest building, its best hotels. It has the stockyards and the Merchandise Mart, a financial center that almost rivals New York. It's a center for advertising and for entertainment, not to mention printing and manufacturing. It produces almost as much steel as Pittsburgh, it's the biggest railroad center in the world and the largest port on the Great Lakes.

But it's more than all that, of course. It has a frontier spirit that shows up in its friendly, eager people. It was meant to impress you, and it usually succeeds. Even Rudyard Kipling, for all he didn't like about Chicago, was forced to say:

"I have struck a city . . . a real city . . . and they call it Chicago. The other places do not count."

Calder's "Red Flamingo" sculpture rises with striking boldness from the Federal Center Plaza right.

It was with some justification, as the views on these pages illustrate, that Chicago's architectural renaissance following the Great Fire of 1871, earned it the title of the 'Birthplace of modern architecture.' The invention of the mechanical elevator, which made tall buildings feasible, brought with it countless skyscrapers, among them Sears Tower above left, which at 1,468 feet, is the world's tallest building.

Coated in bronze-tinted glass and punctuated with light, the Sears Tower *above and right soars into the night sky. Its Wacker Drive lobby* left and below *is decorated with a moving wall sculpture by the famous sculptor and inventor of kinetic art, Alexander Calder, who conceived his 'Universe' of seven elements – a spine, three flowers, helix, pendulum, and sun – each driven by its own motor. Viewed from above overleaf, the United States' second largest city sprawls into the far distance.*

Chicago is the only inland city with combined lake, river and ocean traffic. Its shoreline on Lake Michigan on these pages, is dotted with yacht harbors, sandy beaches and beautiful parks, and Chicago Harbor above and right serves as a picturesque backdrop for the tall buildings which form the spectacular central city skyline.
By night overleaf, the lights of the city cast their reflections on the calm waters of North Lake Shore.

Sight-seeing launches on the Chicago River below
provide an ideal means of viewing some of the city's
most fascinating buildings, among them the
Wrigley Building left, above and right with its
finger-like clock tower.
Beginning just north of the river, "Magnificent
Mile" overleaf is lined with buildings in a unique
variety of revivalist and contemporary architectural
styles.

Reminiscent of ancient Persia, from where the religion originated, the exquisite dome of the Baha'i House of Worship *above* rises from beautiful, secluded gardens, set back from the major highways and expressways *left*, which have made Chicago the "crossroads of America." North Lake Shore Drive *below* carries a relentless stream of traffic along the water's edge.

Soldier Field *right* was originally constructed as a war memorial and later remodeled to provide a magnificent base for the Chicago Bears football team.

Chicago Harbor *overleaf* provides a sheltered haven for innumerable small pleasure craft.

Michigan Avenue below and below left *displays its assembly of spectacular buildings, now the familiar landmarks of a city which is a vast outdoor museum of architecture. The Standard Oil Building* above left *and seen* left *towering above Grant Park, is another striking tribute to modern design. "Big Stan", as this 80-story, steel structure finished in gray marble is affectionately called, is one of the world's tallest buildings. In Grant Park the Buckingham Memorial Fountain* above, right *and overleaf, modeled from one of the Versailles fountains, is about twice the size of its model. From its central stream, 133 jets of water reach two hundred feet into the air.*

40

Chicago is nineteen percent park and playground.
South Lake Drive left provides a walk covered
by intertwining boughs, and Grant Park above
is an immense green expanse loosely following the
pattern of Versailles. In a setting of trees and
shrubs stand a number of fine statues, the most
famous being the magnificent seated Lincoln
right, the last work of Augustus St. Gaudens.
The entrance overleaf is to the Adler
Planetarium, a domed granite structure,
constructed in 1931 and named after its donor,
Max Adler.

43

Between 1883 and 1893 the "Chicago School of Architecture" was born. During that decade a whole galaxy of buildings appeared, reaching the unprecedented heights of twenty-three stories. Since then buildings of the kind shown on these pages have transformed what was once known as the "toddlin' town" into an architectural showpiece. The Loop overleaf reflects all the vitality of a city reborn.

RANDOLPH ST
VIENNA Pure Beef
Shmendl's
PARK
ONE WAY
PARK
CENTENNIAL
Restaurant
WFYR 103½ FM

Chicago's tradition of architectural inventiveness remains strong. Imaginative design has allowed for every convenience with shopping complexes such as the Century Center *center left*, an underground walkway at the Loop *right* and a vast modern railway terminal at Union Station *below right*.

Yet this is also a city of flowers *top*, where the river bank *left* or one of the city's many attractive plazas *above* give the opportunity to relax. The two-level plaza of the First National Bank, ornamented by a major work of Marc Chagall *below*, also provides an open-air restaurant *top left*.

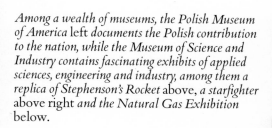

Among a wealth of museums, the Polish Museum of America left documents the Polish contribution to the nation, while the Museum of Science and Industry contains fascinating exhibits of applied sciences, engineering and industry, among them a replica of Stephenson's Rocket above, a starfighter above right and the Natural Gas Exhibition below.

The Dearborn telescope right is displayed in the Adler Planetarium below, which is also the home of the Zeiss cosmic projector center right. The city's oldest museum belongs to the Chicago Historical Society, which celebrated Chicago's business and industrial involvements with the exhibition left.
Skyscrapers line the waterfront overleaf.

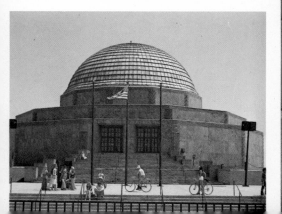

51

Winter strips the foliage from the trees of Chicago's parks and sidewalks and sunlight falls, reflected, on the white marble, stainless steel and tinted glass buildings of the "Queen City of the Lakes." The Chicago River, spanned by numerous bridges, carves its way through the metropolis overleaf.

55

At the southwest edge of the Loop, Sears Tower above rises 109 stories above the Chicago streets, while far below, an old house below right recalls the days which preceded the new building boom. Michigan Avenue left, below and above and center right reflects all the variety and dynamism of a city, which presents a glittering spectacle when viewed by night from the Adler Planetarium overleaf.

In Cominskey Park on these pages *the Chicago White Sox baseball team provides compelling entertainment for thousands of spectators who throng the enormous stadium to watch their favorite players, collect autographs or even enjoy the antics of a jovial clown.*

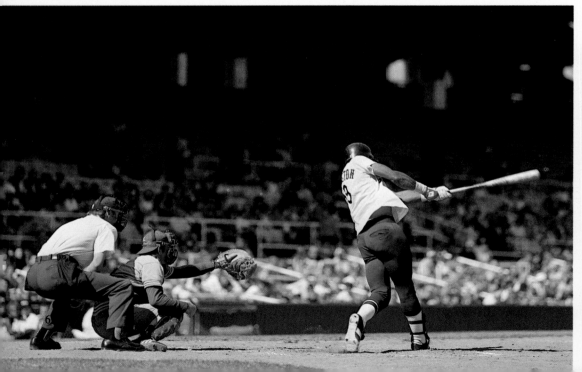

In a strip of architectural virtuosity stand the gleaming white Standard Oil Building above and left *and Lake Point Tower* below and right, *a 70-story building in the shape of a clover leaf. Beside the soaring buildings, the waters of Lake Michigan* above and center right *and the greenery of Grant Park* overleaf *provide a gentle contrast.*

Marina City on these pages includes, in a world-famous complex, apartments, garages, restaurants, offices, a bank, a television theater, an ice-skating rink and a marina. Inside its spectacular twin towers the first 18 stories provide parking space, the remaining 62 stories of each are apartments. The marina at their base forms part of the Chicago River.
North Lake Shore Drive overleaf provides an ideal spot for relaxation.

Chicago is cut by two branches of the Chicago River *above, below and above and center left.* In order to prevent the pollution of Lake Michigan a remarkable engineering feat has reversed the river's natural flow and earned it the title of the "river that flows backwards." North of it, the Ogden Slip Canal *below left also gives access to* the harbor. Downtown Chicago *right presents a* rich variety of contrasting architectural styles and in the heart of it, LaSalle Street *overleaf is the* Wall Street of the Midwest, the site of the city's major banks.

COOK'S
MART
LTD.
ALUMINUM
COMPLETE
GOURMET
TraveLodge
year-round POOL
TAX
undercurrents
waterbeds

The Water Tower above and right *was built two years before the Great Fire as an artistic disguise for a standpipe. Today this fantastic pseudo- Gothic creation remains, surrounded by spectacular skyscrapers, as one of Chicago's most famous landmarks.*

Water Tower Place left and below *is an imaginative structure which includes within its marble walls the Ritz Carlton Hotel, luxury apartments, offices and shops.*

At dusk the sharp profiles of the city skyline overleaf are softened by the half light.

Set back from the shoreline of Lake Michigan above, *the Baha'i House of Worship* right and below *was built by the followers of Baha'u'llah, founder of the Baha'i Faith. Symbolizing the basic principle of the oneness of God, religion and mankind, the temple is a nine-sided structure, partially walled with glass and surmounted by a glorious dome.*
The Chicago campus of the Northwestern University left *includes the medical, dental and law schools of one of the nation's leading private universities.*

The University of Chicago above right occupies a campus of 125 acres. Like the Northwestern University Complex left, above and below, it includes both modern and older buildings and in common with Chicago's many other institutions of learning, among them the Widebold Hall University Complex left, above and below, it offers spacious grounds in which students can pass the time in the manner of students the world over. In summer the meticulously kept flowerbeds of Grant Park overleaf are resplendent with blooms.

83

The 900 apartments of Lake Point Tower above and below right *are sheathed in a glass which becomes almost mirror-like under the rays of the sun. At its feet is an ever popular 'Big Wheel,' which together with other attractions provided by the Chicagofest on this page, offers all the traditional entertainment of the fun fair. Fishing is a popular pastime on the shores of Lake Michigan overleaf.*

The trading floor of the Mercantile Exchange on West Jackson Boulevard these pages is one of the particular fascinations of Chicago. Here the brokers trade in an amazing variety of goods ranging from live cattle to eggs! As orders are taken, the broker reports the price changes to a price reporter, who programs the central computer accordingly. The result is an efficient, streamlined trading system. Expressways and imaginative planning overleaf have assisted the city's development as an industrial, cultural and financial center.

Lincoln Park with its conservatory gardens left is renowned for its seasonal flower displays and for its zoo which features a wide range of animal life including the sea lions in their carefully maintained pit above. The life size model of a squid below is suspended from the ceiling of the John G. Shedd Aquarium as part of a fascinating exhibition of more than 10,000 sea creatures.

The Chicago Temple Building, standing 555 feet high in Gothic revival style, provides space for offices and for a downtown Methodist church of which the magnificent interior can be seen right. Equally splendid is the entrance to the Preston Bradley Hall in the Public Library above right. Its elaborate mosaics and coffered ceiling form a decorative tribute to revivalist architecture.

First published 1980 by Colour Library International Ltd.
© 1980 Illustrations and text: Colour Library International Ltd., 163 East 64th St., New York, N.Y. 10021.
Colour separations by FERCROM, Barcelona, Spain.
Display and text filmsetting by Focus Photoset, London, England.
Printed and bound by JISA-RIEUSSET, Barcelona, Spain.
ISBN 0-8317-1250-3 Library of Congress Catalogue Card No. 79-90596
Published in the United States of America by Mayflower Books, Inc., New York City.

D.L.B. 11958-80